IN HIS SANCTUARY

A MANUAL TO PRESENT BASIC TRUTHS ABOUT JESUS IN HIS SANCTUARY

Compiled by
NORMA GULLY

TEACH Services, Inc.
PUBLISHING
www.TEACHServices.com • (800) 367-1844

Copyright © 2010 Norma Gully & TEACH Services, Inc.
ISBN-13: 978-1-57258-525-6 (Paperback)
Library of Congress Control Number: 2010925072

TEACH Services, Inc.
PUBLISHING
www.TEACHServices.com • (800) 367-1844

GRATEFUL ACKNOWLEDGEMENTS TO:

Pastor Walter Nelson, a well-known and world-traveled evangelist who read the material, and gave valuable input, approved the project, and who, through his influence, opened doors for me to present seminars in the State of Hawaii.

Dr. Douglas Waterhouse, a retired professor of thirty-five years, whose background in Biblical History coupled with his patience and willingness to help, contributed to the accuracy of these materials.

Luevenia Scott, a church elder and experienced Bible instructor, who assisted in the arrangement of the information and encouraged me to present my first seminar.

The many pastors who graciously invited me into their churches and pulpits.

The wonderful people who faithfully supported the seminars with their attendance.

Most of all, the guidance of The Holy Spirit.

DEDICATION

This manual is lovingly dedicated to the memory of my beloved husband, Wilbur Gully, who prayed fervently during its preparation and to our daughters, Denise, Eva, and Lee Kay, whose enthusiasm under girds its pages, and to my spiritual daughter Debbie without whom this work would not have been published.

THE SANCTUARY MADE PLAIN FOR 21ST-CENTURY BELIEVERS

A Seminar by Norma Gully and arranged by Luevenia Scott

This series is written for presentation to Christians of all faiths. Non-Christians can also be brought to Christ through these studies. Its goal is to make the study of the Sanctuary as basic as possible while retaining its deep spiritual truths.

The seminars can be presented in various ways. Some examples are as follows: With an individual or as an interactive group, in a home or church setting, or a Sabbath School or Sunday School setting. The instructor can lead the discussions as the class tolerates. It is imperative that they absorb the material in such a way that the members are able to teach others. Some instructors have taught the class at one session, and then invited class members to teach each other at the next session. In this scenario the instructor is there to answer questions and to clarify points.

It is recommended that the presenter study the material with much prayer. The depths of these sublime truths can only be grasped, even partially, through the ministry of the Holy Spirit. Often, when preparing this material, I felt the awesome presence of God through His Spirit.

My prayer is that fresh glimpses of our beautiful Savior will be seen, and that we will follow Him by faith, as He completes His work for us in the Heavenly Sanctuary.

Sincerely, your servant,
Norma V. Gully
Bible Prophecy Teacher
and Speaker

SANCTUARY SEMINAR
(INTERACTIVE CELL GROUP)
SESSION ONE
WHAT JESUS SAID ABOUT THE SANCTUARY
THE SANCTUARY

THE SANCTUARY

(SECTION 1)

WELCOME

Greet each other and introduce any guests.

Remember to record each other's names and addresses for future reference.

When you were a child, how did you feel about a special person coming to visit your home? Were you excited? Whom did you tell? A neighbor? A classmate? A friend? Your dog or cat?

WORSHIP

Sing together two or three favorite songs or hymns. Take prayer requests. Join hands in a circle of two or three and offer short prayers.

WORD INTRODUCTIONS

Most of us have either heard the story of how God used Moses to deliver His people from the cruel Pharaoh, or perhaps we saw the epic movie *The Ten Commandments*. After this great deliverance, God was excited and happy to have His special family back. So He told Moses to build a Sanctuary because He wanted to dwell among them (Exod. 25:8),—and it was to be patterned after the sanctuary in heaven (Exod. 25:9, 40; Heb. 9:24).

The sanctuary services constituted the way God's people worshipped Him for 1,500 years. A pillar of cloud by day and a pillar of fire by night protected them through their wilderness experience (Exod. 40:37, 38).

THE CHURCH IN THE WILDERNESS

Read Hebrews 9:1–5.

There was a tabernacle in the form of a tent, divided into two apartments and separated by a veil.

List the items recorded in these verses.

1.
2.
3.
4.
5.
6.
7.
8.
9.
10.
11.

In this chapter we see a sand box representation, or type of the work of The Heavenly Trinity, on our behalf.

Please fill in the blanks:

John 8:12 Then spake Jesus unto them saying "I am the _____ of the world." He that followeth me shall not _____ _____ _____."

- What item in the sanctuary represents Jesus in this capacity?

- For you, how is following Jesus like following someone with a light through a dark place?

John 6:35 And Jesus said unto them, "I am the _____ of life. He that cometh to me shall never _____.

- What item in the Sanctuary represents Jesus in this capacity?

- How would you describe your daily spiritual diet? Junk food? Frozen food? Baby food? TV Dinner, Microwaved food? Leftovers? Meat and potatoes? Pure bread and grape juice?

Hebrews 10:16 This is the _____ that I will make with them after those days, saith the Lord: I will put my _____ into their hearts, and in their minds will I write them. See also Psalm 119:32.

- What item (or items) in the Sanctuary is represented in this text? (Heb. 9:4).

- In your daily walk with Jesus, do you sometimes forget that you are in a covenant (binding agreement) relationship with God? Have you attempted to run your own life without "interference" from Him?

Hebrews 7:25 Wherefore He is able also to save them to the uttermost that come unto God by Him, seeing He ever liveth to make _____ for them.

- What item does this scripture allude to? (Heb. 9:4.) See also Revelation 8:3.

- How would your prayer life be affected if you were to keep in mind the close connection of Jesus' very personal intercession for you, and your prayer life? See also Romans 8:26, 27.

Psalm 103:20 Bless the Lord, ye His _____ that excel in strength, that do His commandments, hearkening unto the voice of His word.

- What item in the sanctuary does this scripture describe? (Heb. 9:5.)

- Would there be any changes in your life if you would consciously think more on the fact that we always have heavenly angels as our companions? If so, what would these changes be?

Romans 6:23 The wages of sin is death, but the_____
_____ _____ is _____ _____ through
_____.

- What item in the sanctuary does this scripture describe? (Heb. 9:5.) See also John 3:16.

- Has it been difficult or easy for you to accept this gift? If difficult, why? If easy, why?

Hebrews 10:19, 20 Having therefore, brethren, boldness to enter into the holiest by the blood of Jesus, by a new and living way, which He has consecrated for us _____, that is to say, His _____. Read also John 10:9a. See also Isaiah 53:5, 6; Hebrews 10:4.

- What item in the sanctuary does this scripture describe? (Heb. 9:3).

- Have you ever thought, "Why all this fuss about Jesus? I'm a good person, I love my family, I don't abuse my children, I give to the United Way, I help the sick and the elderly. Surely God will accept me into heaven based on all the good things I do." What's wrong with this picture? Or is there anything wrong with it?

WITNESS

- Share with the group the names of those you have thought about during the week as potential members of this group, so that we can pray for them.

- Remember to pray for each other during the coming week and for our potential members.

SCRIPTURE INDEX—SECTION I

GENERAL INDEX—SECTION I

WELCOME

Greet each other
Introduce any guests.
Hook into the topic by sharing with each other what the word *Sanctuary* means to you. Is it a place to hide? A place to feel safe and snuggly? An escape hatch? Not sure? Something else? Never thought about it?

WORSHIP

Pass out slips of paper. Have each person write down his or her name and one prayer request for the group to pray for during prayer time. Collect the slips and place them in a container.
Sing two or three of your group's favorite songs.
Pass around the container and let each person draw one slip.
Go around the circle and let each person pray for the request of the person whose name they drew. If anyone feels uncomfortable praying aloud, they can say, "I have drawn _____'s name and will pray for him (her) during the week."
Please keep prayers very short (two or three sentences) and pray for only that one request.

WORD

Last week we saw in Exodus 25:8 that God so much wanted to be with His people after He delivered them from Pharaoh's cruel bondage, that He asked Moses to build a sanctuary so He could dwell among them in a special way. This was "church" for God's people for about 1,500 years.
The earthly Sanctuary was a type of the heavenly

Sanctuary, and each item inside and outside represented Jesus. The lampstand represented Jesus, the light of the world. The table of shewbread represented Jesus, the bread of life. The altar of incense represented Jesus placing His righteousness before the Father as our substitute. The Mercy Seat overshadowing the Ten Commandments represented the fact that because of Jesus' death, the penalty for His broken law, which is death (Rom. 3:23; 6:23a), no longer applies to us if we choose Jesus. Yes, God grants us mercy.

WHAT DID JESUS SAY ABOUT THE SANCTUARY?

- Jesus said through one of His Old Testament writers, *"Thy way, O God, is in the sanctuary"* (Ps. 77:13, KJV). (We will endeavor to find some of His ways.)

- Other parts of the Bible also talk about the sanctuary. Read Hebrews 9:6, 7, 8, 9a; Hebrews 8:1, 2. After reading these verses, how would you fill in the blanks below?

   a. The priests went _____ (or daily) into the first compartment.

   b. The high priest went into the second compartment each year.

   c. The earthly sanctuary stood until Jesus began His ministry in the heavenly sanctuary. True or False?

   d. How do you feel about Jesus as our advocate, or go-between, in heaven? Happy? Uncertain? Doesn't have anything to do with me? It's okay for some people? Don't know? Would like to know more? (Circle One)

   Please form into small groups to do the next section

THE OUTSIDE OF THE TABERNACLE

Read each scripture and check off the items as you find them.

- The tabernacle was surrounded by: **An outer courtyard** (Exod. 27:9–18).
  The courtyard represents the earth, where Jesus came to suffer and die for us. There the sinner confesses his sins on the head of an innocent animal and then kills it.

- We see our repentance and confession (1 John 1:9).

- We see Jesus dying for us (Isa. 53:5, 6).

- We see Jesus as the Lamb of God in the innocent animal (John 1:29).

- The tabernacle courtyard contained: **The altar of burnt offering** (Exod. 27:1–7).

    The altar of burnt offering was where the animal was sacrificed.

- It is a voluntary offering (Lev. 1:3).

- It represents Jesus voluntarily dying for us (John 10:18).

- It represents the voluntary offering Jesus expects of us (Rom. 12:1).

Thought Question: Since, obviously, Jesus doesn't expect us to offer our bodies on a real altar to be burned alive, what does it mean when the Bible says we should present our bodies as a living sacrifice?

- The tabernacle courtyard contained: **The lavar** (Exod. 30:18; 38:8).
  The lavar was like a large basin filled with water where

the priests washed their hands and feet before entering the tabernacle. It was situated between the altar of burnt offering and the door into the tabernacle. It symbolized that we should not presume to come into the presence of God with the dust of sin contaminating out hearts.

- The lavar represents the purity of Christ (1 Pet 1:18, 19; John 19:4.)

- Jesus said, "Blessed are the pure in heart" (Matt. 5:8.)

- Jesus said through His prophet Ezekiel, "A new heart also will I give you" (Ezek. 36:26a).

THOUGHT QUESTIONS

- Of course only God knows the true condition of our hearts. But based on the beatitude in Matthew 5:8, how pure do you think your heart is? 100%? 70%? 50%? 25%? Don't know?

- If the Holy Spirit is impressing upon you that there are areas of impurity in your life, what will you do? Ignore them? Excuse them? Say they don't matter as long as I love Jesus? Other?

- The connection between the tabernacle and the courtyard was:

THE DOOR

- Jesus calls Himself the door (John 10:9)

- Jesus said His sheep follow Him, for they know His voice (John 10:4).

- Jesus said that all who came before Him were thieves and robbers, and that sheep do not know the voice of a stranger (John 10:1, 5).

THOUGHT QUESTIONS

- Was there a turning point for you, when you began to hear God's voice?

- How do you discern Jesus' voice over all the other voices that vie for your attention?

- Take with you anything in this lesson that you believe has helped you in your walk with Dear Jesus.

WITNESS

- Share with someone this week any thought you gleaned from the Word this evening.

- Remember to pray for each other and for those you would like to invite to cell group.

SCRIPTURE INDEX—SECTION II

GENERAL INDEX—SECTION II

(SECTION III)

WELCOME

Greet each other.
    Introduce any guests.
    Hook into the topic by sharing what the word "priest"
brings to your mind: Voodoo? Mass? Clergy?

WORSHIP

Sing two or three of the group's favorite songs.
    Join hands in a circle and have each person thank God
for something special they have, and move to the person
to their right (two- or three-sentence prayers, please).

WORD

Last week we again saw Jesus in each item in the
Sanctuary. The outer court represented the earth, where
Jesus came to dwell (tabernacle) among us, (John 1:14).
The Altar of Burnt offering represented the cross, where
Jesus voluntarily laid down His life for us (John 10:18).
    The Lavar, a large basin-like item filled with water,
was where the priests washed their hands and feet before
entering the tabernacle. This water represented the
purity of Jesus. The door into the tabernacle represented
Jesus, the only way we can enter into the presence of
God. Tonight we will study the spiritual significance of
the colors God chose for the Sanctuary (Exod. 28:5).

Gold—Gold has to be heated to remove all of its impurities,
and thus bring out its beauty.

• Jewish history tells us that the gold of the sanctuary,
    after its purification by heat, was beaten, stretched
    into shape and pulled into threads. It was used
    to embroider the curtains, cover the walls of the

14

sanctuary and to construct some of the furniture. See Exodus 28:6, 23, 27 as examples.

- This heating, pulling and stretching is an allegory of suffering. The magnificent beauty of the earthly sanctuary with the candlelight, gorgeous curtains, altar—all reflected in the golden walls like a mirror, along with the red blue, purple and gold of the high priest's attire, was but a dim reflection of Jesus' beauty of character brought out by His suffering.

THOUGHT QUESTIONS

- Have you ever felt like a stranger in the world because of your faith? If so, what types of suffering did you endure?

- In times of personal crisis, do you tend to lean more on God or blame God? Has suffering made you bitter or better?

- Can you see a dim reflection of the suffering of Jesus in your own life? How does this relate to your character development? Read 2 Timothy 3:12 and Revelation 3:18a.

Blue—**Blue** is the color of obedience.

- Read Exodus 24:10 and fill in the blank: "And they saw the God of Israel; and there was under His feet as it were a paved work of a _____ stone."

- Read Exodus 24:12. Many believe that God wrote His Ten Commandments, the foundation of His government, on sapphire stones.

- The blue of the sky and oceans brings to mind the perfect obedience of Jesus to the Ten Commandments of love on **our** behalf.

- The term "true blue" reminds us of the perfect fidelity to God we demonstrate when we obey His commandments.

THOUGHT QUESTIONS

- When you were a child, did the word "obedience" bring positive or negative thoughts to your mind? Explain.

- As you have matured and had the opportunity to observe those around you, do you see a difference in the happiness levels of those who are law-abiding citizens and those who obey only when it suits them? Explain.

- Look back over your life and share with your group some of your happiest moments.

Scarlet—**Scarlet**, or red, is symbolic of blood.

- The red dye used in the sanctuary came from the eggs of an insect called the Scarlet Worm. (The English word "crimson" is derived from the Arabic name of this insect). The insect had to be killed in order to leech the eggs to obtain the dye.

- Jesus calls Himself _____ in Psalm 22:6.

- He was _____ for our transgression, He was _____ _____ for our iniquities (Isa. 53:5).

- Blood is symbolic of the life of the victim, poured out in behalf of the sinner. The Lord uses scarlet, crimson, or red, the color of blood, to alert us to our death-producing sins (Rom. 6:23a).

- Though your sins be as they _____ shall be as white as snow. Though they be like _____ they shall be _____ (Isa. 1:18).

• What two things do you believe God is telling us in the above scripture?

• A-red ray is the first of the rays that light gives off when broken up through a prism. Red reminds us of Jesus, the Light of the World being broken up for us. What thoughts about Jesus does this bring to your mind?

Purple—Purple is the color of royalty and is the combination of the colors red and blue.

• In Bible times, the color purple was obtained by crushing once-living creatures call Murex. They gave off a slime similar to that of snails, which over time and exposure to sunlight gradually changed from white to yellow, green, and finally to purple, which was ineffaceable. This dye was obtained at the cost of the death of thousands of creatures.

• Jesus' life of perfect obedience (blue) blends with the blood of His sacrifice (red) spilled for us on Calvary's cross.

• He then has earned the right to wear purple, the color of royalty. He can now, in His royal, priestly robes, mediate for sinners (us) before God in His celestial sanctuary (Heb. 7:25).

• Jesus has earned the right to be called KING OF KINGS AND LORD OF LORDS (Rev. 19:16).

• When we, as His children, follow Him in love demonstrated by our obedience (John 14:15—blue) and our willingness to shed our blood for Him (Rev.

12:11—red). Then we, too, can wear the robe of royalty purple.

"He hath made us _____ and _____ unto God, His Father (Rev. 1:6)."

White—White represents the purity of Christ.

- The priests had to wear white breeches (undergarments) to cover their reproductive organs. Our reproductive organs are sacred.

- Jesus, the Son of God, was born like any other baby. He came through the birth canal of a woman. The gift of procreation is sacred, which means we must keep our reproductive powers pure before God.

- Jesus was born of a woman without losing one ounce of His purity. During his announcement of Jesus' conception, the Angel Gabriel says, He will be called that holy thing (Luke 1:35). At the beginning of Jesus' ministry, recorded in John 1:29, John the Baptist called Him the Lamb of God. And after Jesus ascended into heaven, Peter expressed in 1Peter 1:18–20 that we are redeemed with the precious blood of Jesus, as of a Lamb without spot or blemish.

- Jesus was born of a woman and maintained His purity all of His life. According to John 1:12, when we, by the power of Christ ministering to us through the Holy Spirit, are born of a spiritual woman, the church, we, too, have power to maintain our spiritual purity.

THOUGHT QUESTIONS

- When you were a child did you ever dream of being a king or queen? What thoughts came to your mind?

- Did you ever think that you are in training to be royalty in Heaven? Why? Why not?

- When Princess Elizabeth and Princess Margaret were little girls in the palace, there was a marked difference in their training. Elizabeth was trained to be a Queen, and she is now the reigning monarch of Great Britain. Since we are in training to be royalty, what are some ways in which we can demonstrate this in our everyday lives?

Take with you a "gem" from this lesson that you can admire or meditate on during the coming week.

WITNESS

- Think of ways to get others to come to next week's cell meeting. Pray for each other during the week.

FACTS ABOUT THE PRIESTS

Fact #1   The tribe that found favor with God and became the tribe that God used in the Sanctuary Services was the tribe of Levi (Exod. 32:25–28).

Fact #2   The men God selected to be priests and minister before Him were Aaron and his sons (Exod. 28:1; 30:30).

Fact #3   The priest's clothing was designed by God (Exod. 28:1–4).

Fact #4   The colors of the materials were gold, blue, red, white and purple (Exod. 28:5).

Fact #5   The High priest wore a breastplate over his gorgeous clothing, called the breastplate of judgment (Exod. 28:29). Embedded in it were twelve precious stones, each bearing the name of one of the twelve tribes of Israel (Exod. 28:15–29).

Fact #6 The high priest also wore stones called the *Urim* and T*hummin* on each side of the breastplate. These were used to ascertain God's will in a given situation. If God's answer were yes, a light would encircle the Urim on the right side. If no, a shadow came over the Thummin on the left side (Exod. 28:30).

Fact #7 The high priest wore the white clothing of the common priest during the daily services, but wore his gorgeous clothing on the Day of Atonement (Exod. 28, Lev. 16).

Fact #8 The high priest was the only one allowed into the Most Holy Place where the Shekinah Glory overshadowed the Mercy Seat. This occurred only once yearly, on the Day of Atonement. He made special precautions before entering (Lev. 16:2).

Fact #9 The priests were teachers of the people. They mediated in civil matters, made decisions about heath matters, received portions of the sacrifices, were paid by the tithe, and received special offerings.

Fact #10 The entire tribe of Levi was used in the upkeep of the temple. Only the high priests could enter it. They had to cover the sacred articles before the regular Levites could transport them. The Ark of the Covenant was always transported on the shoulders of the priests in advance of the people.

SCRIPTURE INDEX—SECTION III

Read Exodus chapter 28; p. 20
     28:1—p. 19
     28:1–4—p. 19
     28:5—p. 14, 19
     28:6, 23, 27—p. 15
     28:15–29—p. 19
     28:29—p. 19
     28:30—p. 20
     30:12–16—p. 15
     30:30—p. 19
     32:25–28—p. 19

Leviticus
Read Leviticus 16—p. 20
     16:2—p. 20

Psalms
     22:6—p. 16

Isaiah
     1:18—p. 17
     53:5—p. 16

Luke
     1:35—p. 18

John
     1:12—p. 18
     1:14—p. 14
     1:29—p. 18
     10:18—p. 14
     14:15—p. 17

Romans
     6:23a—p. 16

2 Timothy
     3:12—p. 15

GENERAL INDEX—SECTION III

(SECTION IV)

WELCOME

Greet each other, welcome guests.

Hook into the topic by defining what *sacrifice* means to you. Does true sacrifice have to hurt?

WORSHIP

Sing a few songs of the group's choosing.

Take prayer requests.

Break up into groups of two or three. Spend three to seven minutes praying for requests.

WORD

Last week we discovered some beautiful spiritual lessons concealed in the colors God chose for the earthly sanctuary. In this study we will uncover lessons of truth buried in the daily services of the sanctuary.

Break up into small groups. When you have found the answers in the scriptures, please place a check mark by your answer.

THE BURNT OFFERING

The Burnt Offering is found in Leviticus 1, and stood for an entire surrender of the life to God.

- It had to be a male without blemish, and a voluntary offering. Read Leviticus 1:3.

- Jesus was without blemish (1Peter 1:18,19).

- Jesus voluntarily laid down His life for us (John 10:13, 17, 18). Share with your group what Jude 24 means to you.

23

The fire which God Himself kindled, consumed the sacrifice. Read Leviticus 9:24.

- The work of the Holy Spirit is to consume sin in our lives. Read Zechariah 4:6 and John 16:8.

- How do you feel about the Holy Spirit working in your life: A little afraid? Glad? Eager to get it over with?

The blood of the animal had to be sprinkled. Read Leviticus 1:5, 11, 15.

- The life is in the blood, which represents Jesus' ability, by reason of His pure, spotless life, to cleanse us from all sin. Read Leviticus 17:11; 1 Peter 1:18, 19 and 1 John 1:7.

- Why do you think there was so much killing of animals in the sanctuary service? Wouldn't it have been enough to inflict a wound of some type on the animal and catch that blood and sprinkle it on the places directed by God?

God is no respecter of persons. Read Colossians 3:24, 25.

- He made provision for all economic classes to offer sacrifices. Read Leviticus 1:2,10,14.

- Do you think that God looks with more favor on the size of the offering, or on the motive that prompted it? Why?

THE MEAL OFFERINGS

The meal offerings are found in Leviticus 2. (*Meal* is a more correct translation of the word *meat* as used in this chapter from the King James Bible).

The meal offerings represented Jesus, the **Bread of Life**. He is the sustainer of all life, and the meal offerings were an acknowledgement of our total dependence on God. Read John 6:48.

- No leaven was to be used in the meal offerings because leaven usually represents sin. Read Leviticus 2:11; Luke 12:1; 1 Corinthians 5:8.

- Based on your knowledge of baking, what do sin and leaven have in common?

In order for bread to give life, the reproductive powers of the wheat are destroyed by grinding it into meal, so it can be made into bread to feed the world's hungry.

- Just as the seed must die before a new life can spring up, Jesus had to die so that He could offer eternal life to the world. Read John 3:16.

- Read Galatians 2:20, and share with your group what you think Paul is talking about when he says he "is crucified with Christ."

THE PEACE OFFERINGS

The peace offerings are found in Leviticus 3. They were used for:

- Thank offerings or praise offerings (Lev. 7: 12, 15).

- Offerings when a vow was made (Lev. 7:16). A communal offering (Deut. 12:17, 18).

THE SIN OFFERINGS

- The sin offerings were for sins of ignorance, errors, mistakes, and rash acts. Read Leviticus 4:2, 13, and Numbers 15:24–29.

- They were not for sins committed knowingly, defiantly, or persistently. Read Numbers 15:32–36.

They are listed as follows:

- For the anointed priest. Read Leviticus 4:3–12.

- For the whole congregation. Read Leviticus 4:13–21.

- For a ruler. Read Leviticus 4:22–26.

- For a common person. Read Leviticus 4:27–31.

THOUGHT QUESTION

- Since God is no respecter of persons, why do you think He had different offerings for different groups of people?

Take with you a thought to share with someone this week.

WITNESS

Prepare to share with the group the name of someone you asked to join us next week, and what they said or did when you invited them.

Remember to pray for each other during the week.

FACTS ABOUT THE DAILY SERVICES

Fact # 1   The sinner brought the required animal to the outer court of the Sanctuary. He confessed his sin on its head while pressing down, thus, in type, transferring his sin to the animal. (The animal could be a bullock, sheep, or goat. In certain situations turtledoves or grain was used, with a few variations.)

Fact #2   The sinner kills the animal by slitting its throat. The priest catches its blood in a basin. The blood represented Jesus' blood, which would one day be shed for the whole world.

Fact #3 The priest takes the blood into the Holy Place (first room in the sanctuary), dips his thumb into the blood, and leaves a thumbprint on the horns of the Altar of Incense. Thus, he transfers the sins of the individual to the sanctuary itself. This showed that the wages of sin (death), for God's broken law, had been exacted.

Fact #4 Sometimes the priest sprinkled the blood of the animal on or before the veil that separated the Holy Place from the Most Holy Place.

Fact #5 At times the flesh of the animal would be burned upon the Altar of Burnt Offering. The fat was always to be burned before the Lord, because it represented sin. (The priest was never to eat it.) The priest would eat a tiny piece of the meat, in type transferring the sins to himself. This represented the priest as carrying the sins of the people in type, as Jesus actually carries our sins.

Fact #6 There were also the morning and evening sacrifices, which the priests offered daily, showing God's mercy and grace over the camp even before the individuals brought their sacrifices.

Fact #7 The daily services of the sanctuary went on for an entire year. They were called the *ha-tamid*. Then, once a year, on the Day of Atonement (At-One-Ment, also called "Cover-up Day," or *Yom Kippur*, the sins of the people were removed from the sanctuary during a special service. This service is outlined in Leviticus, 16, which we will focus on at our next meeting.

SCRIPTURE INDEX—SECTION IV

GENERAL INDEX—SECTION IV

(SECTION V)

WELCOME

Greet each other. Share with each other your experiences when you invited others to church.

Hook into topic by sharing how you felt when you received a court summons. If you've never received one, how do think you would feel?

WORSHIP

Sing a few songs of the group's choosing.

Join hands in a circle and ask one or two people to pray for the presence of the Holy Spirit.

WORD

Last week we discovered lessons in the daily sacrifices of the earthly sanctuary that we can apply to our lives now. Tonight we will look at:

Book – *The Earthly Day of Atonement*.
Read Leviticus 16.

LOOK

The Day of Atonement (Day of At-one-ment) is called *Yom Kippur*

Cover-Up Day occurred once a year on the tenth day of Tishri,the seventh day of month of the Jewish calendar of that day. This month corresponds to our September/ October (verse 29).

- What does the fact that the Day of Atonement took place once a year (verse 34) tell you of its importance? Write your answer here.

_____

_____

_____

- What does the fact that the Day of Atonement had to be repeated every year tell you about human nature?

THE PREPARATIONS OF THE HIGH PRIEST

Read verse 4. Write in your own words what it says.

_____

_____

_____

- Why do you think that God was so particular about the washing? What do you think the white of the High Priest's attire represented?

- In what ways might this instruction to the High Priest regarding cleanliness apply to hygiene today?

Read verses 12 and 13. Write in your own words what they say.

_____

_____

_____

- Do you sometimes feel that your sins are odious to God? (They stink.) Do you see a relationship to this feeling and the incense used in the services? Explain.

Read verses 6, 11, and 14. Here we see the high priest taking a bullock and offering its blood for his own sins and the sins of his household.

- What does this tell you about the nature of the earthly high priest?

• Contrast the nature of the high priest with that of Jesus, our Heavenly High Priest (1 Peter 1: 18, 19).

• The high priest was a man who, by reason of his office, had a deeper knowledge and experience of the holy things than the average person, and yet had to offer a sin offering. What does that show us about our relationship to Jesus, our sin offering? Write your answers below.

a.

b.

c.

THE LORD'S GOAT

Lots were cast upon two goats. The goat upon which the Lord's lot fell was designated "The Lord's Goat" Read verses 7–9.

• Read verse 15 and write what was done in the Most Holy Place with the Lord's goat, also called the sin offering. Write your answer here.

_____
_____
_____

• No sins were confessed over the Lord's goat. What aspect of Christ's life and ministry does this goat represent? Write your answer here. Read 1 Peter 1:18, 19.

_____
_____
_____

- Sins were confessed on the bullock. What aspect of Christ's life does this convey? Write your answer here. Read Isaiah 53:6.

_____

_____

_____

- List other places where the blood of the Lord's goat, or sin offering, was offered. Read verses 16, 18, 19.

    1.

    2.

- Note in verse 18 that the blood of the goat and the bullock were offered together in answer # 2. Jewish history tells us they were mixed together. Who do both sacrifices represent? Write your answer here.

_____

_____

_____

THE SCAPEGOAT

A lot fell on another goat, designating him as the scapegoat. Read verses 7, 8, 10.

At the end of the reconciling of the Most Holy Place, the Holy Place, and the Altar of Burnt Offering, the high priest transferred the sins of the congregation to the scapegoat (verses 20, 21).

The scapegoat shall do what with the iniquities of the children of Israel? Read verse 22. Write your answer here.

_____

_____

_____

- Who do you think this scapegoat represents? Why? Write your answer here.

_____
_____
_____

• The camp is clean. Read verses 30–34.

• The attitude of the people during the Day of Atonement. Read verse 29.

• The blood of the Lord's Goat (sin offering) had cleansed the camp "in type." Read Hebrews 10:1–4. But could the blood of animals ever really make a person clean? Write your answer here.

_____
_____
_____

• Leviticus 17:11 tells us that the life is in the blood and makes atonement for the soul. Read Hebrews 9:14, 26, 28 and 10:14.In what way is Jesus' blood superior to that of animal sacrifices? Write your answer here.

_____
_____
_____

• Share with your group about the time you first recognized the power of Jesus' blood in your life. Take with you a thought to share with a family member or friend this week.

WITNESS

• Pray for each other during this coming week. Plan an outreach program for your group.

FACTS ON EARTHLY DAY OF ATONEMENT—LEVITICUS 16

FACT #1 The Day of Atonement occurred on the tenth day of the Jewish month, which is named

Tishri. This corresponds to our September/ October (verse 29).

FACT #2 On the Day of Atonement, also called *Yom Kippur,* the records of the sins of the people which had been piling up all year would be removed, and the camp would be clean (verses 30–34).

FACT #3 The High Priest placed a censer of hot coals, which were taken from the Altar of Incense before the Mercy Seat in the Most Holy Place. The Incense covered the Mercy Seat so that he would not die when he went in to perform the services (verses 12, 13).

FACT #4 Earlier, he had confessed his sins on the head of a bullock, and killed it. He now goes into the Most Holy Place and sprinkles the blood on and before the Mercy Seat as the Lord directed (verses 11, 14).

FACT #5 The goats were selected by bringing two of the animals before the Lord, and having the High Priest cast lots upon them. The goat on which one lot fell was called the Lord's goat (Verses 7–9). The goat on which the other lot fell was called the scapegoat.

FACT #6 He killed the Lord's goat and did the same with its blood as with the blood of the bullock (verse 15).

FACT #7 Next, he placed the blood of the bullock and the goat upon the horns of the Altar of Incense in the Holy Place (verse 16).

FACT #8 Then he put the blood of both animals on the horns of the altar of burnt offering (verses 18, 19).

FACT #9 After blessing the people, he placed the sins of the congregation upon the head of the scapegoat, which represents Satan, the originator of all sin (verses 21, 22).

SCRIPTURE INDEX-SECTION V

GENERAL INDEX—SECTION V

(SECTION VI)

WELCOME

Greet each other with a hug or a handshake.
Hook into topic by sharing how you feel about actually
seeing Jesus face to face.

WORSHIP

Sing "Face to Face" from the church hymnal.
Sing two or three choruses praising Jesus.
Kneel for prayer in groups of two or three.

WORD

Last week we looked at the earthly Day of Atonement
and discovered lessons about our lovely Savior, Jesus.
Tonight we will look for parallels in the heavenly Day of
Atonement to assist us in understanding what Jesus is
doing for us now.

Book — *The Heavenly Day of Atonement*

LOOK

THE DATES FOR THE EARTHLY AND HEAVENLY DAYS OF ATONEMENT

The earthly Day of Atonement took place on the tenth
day of the seventh month of the Jewish calendar, which
corresponds to our September/October (Lev. 16:29).

The heavenly Day of Atonement began on October 22,
1844. (In an earlier lesson we computed the date. If you
were not in this cell group at this time, refer to page 44,
last paragraph, for the calculation.)

CONFESSED SINS

The daily confessed and forgiven sins were transferred to the earthly sanctuary via the blood of the slain animals. (See Facts on the Earthly Day of Atonement.)

Our confessed sins are recorded in heaven via the blood of Jesus. (Read 1 John 1:7 and 1 John 1:9.)

- Looking back over your life, do you think your sins would probably fill a sandwich bag? A trash can? A garbage can? A dump truck? The Pacific Ocean?

- If the Holy Spirit brings to your mind some sin you haven't confessed to our dear Jesus, why not bow your head and silently confess it to Him now?

COVER-UP DAY

On the earthly Day of Atonement the blood of the Lord's goat covered up the records of the forgiven sins of the people at the end of the service. The camp was clean. Read Leviticus 16:15, 16, 18, 30, 33.

- Today, during the real or antitypical Day of Atonement, the blood of Jesus is covering up/blotting out the records of all of our confessed sins. Read Isaiah 43:25 and 1 John 1:7.

- Soon He will come for us. Everyone will have made his or her final choice (Rev. 22:11, 12.). And He will come without sin (Heb. 9:26, 28) for those of us who are looking for Him.

During the covering up, or blotting out, time, Jesus is purifying us by His blood through the mighty agency of the third person of the Godhead, the Holy Spirit. (Read John 16:7–14, Ezekiel 36:26, 27, Hebrews 8:10,1 John 1:7, Jude 1:24.)

- Do you live your life as if you were being made holy?

- In what way is God calling you to practice greater holiness?

A PEN PICTURE OF THE BEGINNING OF THE JUDGMENT (THE HEAVENLY DAY OF ATONEMENT).

READ DANIEL 7: 9,10,13,14,22,27.

Please fill in the blanks.

- The Ancient of Days is _____. Read Psalms 90:2 and 103:19.

- Thousands upon thousands _____ attend this tribunal. Read Daniel 7:10 and Psalm 103:20, 21.

- Comes to the Ancient of Days to engage in the last acts of His heavenly ministration on our behalf (Dan. 7:13, 14, Hebrews 7:25).

- He will perform the work of investigative judgment and will make atonement for those entitled to its benefits (Heb. 9: 26–28).

- The kingdoms of this world will be given to us (Dan, 7:22, 27).

- Compare appearing in an earthly court setting to appearing in absentia in a heavenly court setting.

THE RECORD BOOKS IN HEAVEN

(Dan. 7:10b last part)

* The book of life. (Rev. 20:12; Luke 10:20).

  Only those whose names are written in the book of life will be in heaven.

* The book of remembrance. Read Mal. 3:16, Ps. 56:8.

* Record of sins (Isa. 65:6, 7).

  What type of records do you think are written in heaven about you?
  If you could change one thing about your life, what would it be?

THE LAW OF GOD

The law of God is the standard by which all will be judged. (Eccl. 12:13, 14 and James 2:12).

* If you could change one of God's laws, which one would it be?

* Why?

  Jesus is our only hope.

* Jesus kept His Father's commandments and will give us power to obey them (John 1:12).

* The righteousness of the law will be fulfilled (filled up) in those of us who are led by the Holy Spirit. (Rom. 8:1–4, 14).

* He, Jesus, is living in us through the Holy Spirit (Gal.

2:20, Rev. 3:20).

- Now Jesus, our Heavenly Advocate (High Priest) is able to save us to the uttermost. Read Hebrews 7:25. And He will present us faultless by His blood. Read Jude 1:24 and 1 John 1:7.
- The final decision in each case will be made by Jesus Himself, the One who suffered such a painful death for us (John 5:22; Isa. 53:5, 6).

- Beloved, remember that just as the earthly high priest carried the names of the Tribes of Israel on the precious stones in the breastplate, so Jesus carries us, His precious stones, in the heavenly breastplate right over His heart.

Do you believe that God has been fair in His dealings with you during your life? Or do you think He is too hard on you at times?

What will be some of the joys of living in a sin-free environment, in your opinion?

WITNESS

- Share With Others The Joy Of Our Savior's Soon Coming

THE TIME OF THE JUDGMENT

- In Daniel 8:14 the Bible makes a prophecy that the Sanctuary would be cleansed after 2300 days. (Note: A prophetic day is equal to one literal year (Ezek. 4:6), so this is a 2300 literal-year prophecy.

- This cleansing was always performed on the Day of Atonement by the High Priest in Israel (Lev. 16:29, 30; 23:27).

- This cleansing was the removal of sin that had been recorded in the Sanctuary through the daily services (Lev. 16:16).

- If the people of Israel or individuals did not participate correctly on that day, then they would be cut off, or destroyed (Lev. 23:29, 30). (Note: The Day of Atonement was a type of judgment.)

- This cleansing was only a shadow, or symbol, of the real cleansing that would take place in heaven by our High Priest, Jesus (Heb. 9:24).

- Jesus cleanses the heavenly Sanctuary by the removing of all sin that's been confessed and forsaken through the investigative judgment process (Heb. 9:25–27).

- The 2300 days tells us when this investigative judgment began (Dan. 9:23–25). (Note: It began when the decree to rebuild Jerusalem was given, in 457 B.C.)

- Daniel 9:25 says that after seven and sixty-two prophetic weeks (69 weeks, or 483 years), Jesus would begin His earthly ministry. (Note: Jesus began in the fall of A. D. 27, when He was baptized by John.)

- Daniel 9:26, 27 says that in the middle of the last prophetic week, the 70th, Jesus would be cut off. (Note Jesus died exactly three and a half years—half a week—on the cross, in A. D. 31. Three and a half years later the prophetic weeks end, in A. D. 34.

- The 70 weeks, or 490 prophetic days/literal years, were cut off from the 2300-day vision of Daniel 8:14. (See Daniel 9:21–23.) This leaves 1,810 years. To find out when the 2,300 days ends, we add the remaining 1,810 years onto A. D. 34 and we come to 1844. This is the year Jesus began cleansing the heavenly sanctuary. This is when He began the real time of judgment, of which the earthly Day of Atonement was just a symbol.

```
   2300        -original prophecy
minus 490 years -given to Jewish nation
   1810        -years remaining in original prophecy
plus    34 A.D.  -end of 490 years
   1844        -the judgment began in heaven
```

SCRIPTURE INDEX—SECTION VI

GENERAL INDEX—SECTION VI

PRAYING THROUGH THE SANCTUARY

THE OUTER COURT

In the outer court the sinner repents of his sins and asks for cleansing (The Laver). Then he confesses his sins on the head of his animal sacrifice, which he kills. Since the wages of sin is death, the animal has died in his place. In our prayer, we should humble our hearts realizing that our sins have caused the death of Jesus.

Step One: *Confess our sins*

The Holy Place (first compartment)

Where the blood containing the record of sins (in type) is taken by the priest and placed on the horns of the altar of incense. The incense ascends upward and over the two compartments, and is wafted towards the mercy seat.

In prayer, through the Holy Spirit, and by faith we can leave our sins in the Holy Place. Jesus takes our prayers and sprinkles them with His blood, then mixes them with the incense of His righteousness, and presents them to our Heavenly Father, who lovingly answers them.

Step Two: *Ask for the continued intercession of Jesus in your life (the altar), for your daily needs to be provided (the Shewbread), and for the Holy Spirit to continue His work in your life (the Candlesticks).*

The Most Holy Place (second compartment)

On the Day of Atonement, the blood of the Lord's goat cleanses the sanctuary of all the sins of the people, when it is sprinkled on and before the mercy seat. At the same time, the people are humbling their hearts.

In prayer we can ask for total cleansing from our sins as we seek to obey all of His commandments (the Ten

Commandments). While at the same time we can ask to be covered with God's mercy (the Mercy Seat) as we are protected by the Holy Angels (the Angels).

Step Three: *Ask for total cleansing from sin and for His protection and mercy as we seek to cooperate with the Holy Spirit in the special work of purification required by God in preparation for translation.*

Bringing It All Together (Part 1)

SHADOWS OF HIS SACRIFICE

[After sin entered this earth, animal sacrifices were offered to remind God's people that one day Jesus would come and pay the wages of sin (death). Examples: God's slaying an animal in the Garden of Eden; Cain and Abel, Abraham, Noah, and others who offered animal sacrifices. This system existed for about 2,500 years].

[From the time of Moses to Christ's day, the Sanctuary was made the center of worship].

After Jesus died, was resurrected, and returned to heaven, He began His ministry for us in the Heavenly Sanctuary, of which the earthly sanctuary was a type, or pattern (Exod. 25: 9, 40; Heb. 9:24).

It is interesting to note that God has always maintained contact with His earthbound children.

It is also interesting to note the importance of the sanctuary. It is referred to in half of the book of Exodus, all of Leviticus, a third of the book of Numbers, and some of Deuteronomy. It is also alluded to in the Psalms and Prophets. The Sanctuary is found in almost all of Hebrews, alluded to in other books of Paul, and in every chapter of the book of Revelation.

THE EARTHLY SANCTUARY

- The Sanctuary was situated in the middle of the camp and was surrounded by a courtyard.

- The large altar is called THE ALTAR OF BURNT OFFERING (Exod. 27:1–8).

- Between the Altar of Burnt Offering and the tent is the Lavar. Exodus 40:7; 30:17–21.

- The curtains and veils are found in Exodus 38:9–20.
- The sinner brings his sacrifice, which represents Jesus (John 1:29).

THE HOLY PLACE AND MOST HOLY PLACE

Daily services were performed in the outer courtyard and in the first room, or apartment. Then, once a year, on the Day of Atonement, a special service was performed by the High Priest, who could enter the Most Holy place only after following God's explicit directions (Lev. 16).

- The Holy Place is described in Hebrews 9:1, 2.

- The Most Holy Place is described in Hebrews 9:3, 4, 5.

THE HOLY PLACE CONTAINED:

- The Seven-branch Candlestick (Exodus 40:2–25; 57, 17, 24) represented Jesus, the Light of the World (John 1:9).

- The bread upon the Table of Shewbread (Exodus 25:23–30; 40:23) represented Jesus, the Bread of Life (John 6:35, 38).

- The Altar of Incense, also called the Altar of Intercession (Exodus 30:1–10), represents Christ's breath of intercession for us (Rom. 8:26). Jesus can intercede for us *only* because of His perfect righteousness (1 Peter 1:18, 19; Heb. 7:25). The incense also represents His righteousness, which makes our prayer acceptable to God. In Revelation 5:8, the odors/incense refer to the prayers of the saints (us).

THE MOST HOLY PLACE CONTAINED:

The Ark of the Covenant (Exod. 25:9–17), with Aaron's

rod that budded; the golden pot of manna; the tables of the covenant (Ten Commandments); and the Mercy Seat with an angel on either side.

THE MERCY SEAT

The glory of God shone from the Mercy Seat between the two angels. The Mercy Seat was above the Ten Commandments. The light shining from the Mercy Seat was called the SHEKINAH GLORY.

THE TEN COMMANDMENTS

The Ten Commandments define the law of God just as a prism breaks down the sunlight into the beautiful colors of the rainbow, and His law of love is the standard by which we shall be judged (James 2:10–12; John 14:15).

Just as God's glory was manifested between the angels or cherubims in the Most Holy Place of the earthly sanctuary, so He dwells between the cherubims in heaven (Ps. 80:1).

God's glory is His character of love defined in the Ten Commandments (Exod. 33:17–19; John 14:15). Therefore, when He writes His laws in our hearts (Ezek. 36:26, 27; Heb. 10:16, 17), He makes it possible for us to be reflectors of His glory. BEHOLD WHAT MANNER OF LOVE THE FATHER HAS BESTOWED UPON US THAT WE SHOULD BE CALLED THE SONS OF GOD! (1 John 3:1). WE CANNOT FATHOM THIS LOVE, ONLY SEEK TO BEHOLD IT!

THE SERVICES OF THE COURTYARD REPRESENTED:

Our repentance and confession. [The sinner placed his hand on the head of the offering without blemish, which represented Jesus, the Lamb of God, and pressed down, in type transferring his sins to the animal, that would die in his place just as Jesus would one day die in his place, the antitype (John 1:29; 1Peter 1:18,19)].

The priest, who took the blood into the Sanctuary,

represented Jesus, our Heavenly High Priest, who ministers His own blood for us (Heb. 7:25; 9:12 & 24). We must, by faith place our sins upon Jesus and leave them there.

The services on the Day of Atonement in the Most Holy Place represented the final end of sin in our lives and in the universe.

Jesus offers us not only forgiveness of sin, but also cleansing from *all* unrighteousness (1 John 1:9). *He* is *able* to present us faultless before His presence with exceeding joy (Jude 24).

THE SPIRITUAL LESSONS OF THE SACRIFICES

The morning and evening sacrifices were offered continually before the Lord (Num. 28:2, 3, 6, 8). They stood for the continual effectiveness of Christ's sacrifice. Because of Jesus' sacrifice of Himself, the whole world is covered by His grace. This gives people opportunity to accept Him, and is the reason evil is not always immediately destroyed by God (2 Peter 3: 9, 10;Eccles. 8:11).

THE DAILY PERSONAL OFFERINGS:

- THE BURNT OFFERING-Leviticus 1 (Entire Surrender to God).

- THE MEAL OFFERING-Leviticus 2 (Total Dependence on God).

- THE PEACE OFFERINGS-Leviticus 3 (Thanks and praise to God).

- THE SIN OFFERINGS-Leviticus 4 (Sins of error, ignorance).

- THE TRESPASS OFFERING-Leviticus 5 (Assorted mistakes).

Bringing It All Together (Part 2)

THE CROSS SEEN IN THE LAYOUT OF
THE WILDERNESS SANCTUARY

THE CROSS

- The ark of the testament is at the top of the cross.

- The Seven-Branched Candlestick is on the left-hand arm of the cross.

- The Table of Shewbread is on the right-hand arm of the cross.

- The altar of incense is between the Seven-branched Candlestick and the Table of Shewbread.

- The laver is below the Altar of Incense on the bottom section of the cross.

- And the Altar of Burnt Offering, which represents the cross where Jesus died, is at the foot of the cross.

- This layout shows us that Jesus had to die in order to minister His own blood for us in the Heavenly Sanctuary Heb. 9:1l,12), and to be able to finally put away sin by the sacrifice of Himself (Heb. 9:26, 28).

THE BEGINNING OF HIS MINISTRY

- Jesus' ministration in the Holy Place began in A. D. 31, when He returned to heaven, and continues for us now in the Most Holy Place of the Heavenly Sanctuary. This judgment began in 1844.

- It is sad to say that the Jewish leaders of Jesus' day had a veil over their eyes because of unbelief. Daily they had sacrificed animals in anticipation of the Messiah coming to die for them, yet they rejected their own Messiah when He did come. You see, deliverance from their yoke of Roman bondage was the focus of their thinking rather than deliverance from their spiritual bondage. And today, the Jewish nation as a whole continues to look for the Messiah.

- A lesson for us is that we, as God's people, should be more interested in being delivered from the yoke of spiritual bondage that is so vividly illustrated in the study of the Heavenly Sanctuary, than in temporal blessings.

- When Moses came down from Mount Sinai after receiving the Ten Commandments, he had to place a veil over his face to protect the people from the reflection of the light that surrounds God, which was reflected in his face. Let not the people of God hide the brightness of God's character by covering it with the rubbish of life. God's brightness, or glory, represents His pure character (Exod. 33: 18, 19; 34:5,–7 and Psalms 104:1 & 2).

THE EARTHLY SANCTUARY AS A TYPE OF THE HEAVENLY SANCTUARY

Type and shadow

- The earthly sanctuary was a type of the Heavenly Sanctuary (Exod. 25: 9, 40), and a shadow of heavenly things –(Heb. 8:5), but it could not of itself make men perfect –(Heb. 10: 9–14.

- By participating in its services, the people showed their faith in Jesus and what He would accomplish for them in the future. That is why the whole round of services was repeated yearly. Jesus, the true Messiah, had yet to come.

THE COVENANTS

THE TWO COVENANTS

A covenant is an agreement between two entities, usually equals.

In the case of God's people, He, the Superior One, condescended to make a covenant with us, the works of His hands. He did this because of His love for us.

- The Sanctuary was an illustration of the old covenant, or temporary covenant the set of promises made by God to man, which ended at the cross (Heb. 8:7–10, John 19:30; Mark 15:37–39)

- After Jesus died and rose from the dead, God entered into a New Covenant relationship with His people— (Heb. 8: 6–12). Actually, this was the original covenant God had made with Adam and Eve in Genesis 3:15. In this covenant we see the power of Christ working in our lives –(Ps. 119:32, Ezek. 36:26, 27, Jude 24; 1 John 1:9; Heb. 10:16, 17, Rev. 14:12). It is called a better covenant because all sins could be forgiven under this covenant. [Some sins were of such a daring and presumptuous nature under the old covenant that there was no atonement specified by law (see Letter 276, 1904).]

- (In the original language, *faith of Jesus* can also be translated as 'faith in Jesus'). Since only those who obey God will enter heaven (Rev. 22:14), and since we, because of our fallen natures, cannot obey Him in our own strength, (Rom.14-21) the only way we can obey Him is by faith in Jesus (Rom. 1:17, 8: 1–4).

- The blood of Jesus is all powerful. In the better covenant we are cleansed from sin by His blood. Perfect obedience has always been the condition by which we may obtain eternal life. Jesus, as the second Adam, obeyed the commandments perfectly, and when we accept Him by faith, He gives us the power to do the same (John 1; 12; read Letter 276, 1904).

THE HEAVENLY SANCTUARY

The Heavenly Sanctuary is a real place (Heb. 8: 1, 2; 9:12; 14), and is involved with the new covenant (Heb 8:8, 10).
  Glimpses of the Sanctuary and its Furniture in the Bible.

• The Candlesticks (Rev. 1:12)

• The Altar of incense (Rev. 8:3)

• The Censer (Rev. 8:3).

• The Most Holy Place and the Ark of His Testament, which contains the Ten Commandments (Rev. 11:19) (The only time the Most Holy Place was "open" in the Earthly Sanctuary, was on the Day of Atonement).

• The Heavenly Day of Atonement began on October 22, 1844, which corresponds to the tenth day of the seventh Jewish month, called *Tishri* (Lev. 16:29).

THE JUDGMENT

"TO SOME, THE CONCEPT OF A REAL JUDGMENT MAY BE NEW".

Some may have heard the word, yet be unclear as to what it really means.
  Some may have never thought of a judgment.

CONTRASTS

• The daily confessed and forgiven sins were transferred to the earthly sanctuary via the blood of the slain animals.

- Our confessed sins are recorded in heaven as forgiven via the blood of Jesus (1 John 1:7, 9).

- On the "Earthly Day of Atonement" the blood of the Lord's goat covered up the records of the forgiven sins of the people (The Day of Atonement was called Yom Kippur, or cover-up day).

- Today, during the real, or antitypical, "Day of Atonement", the blood of Jesus, our perfect sacrifice, is covering up/removing from heaven the record of all our sins (Isa. 43:25).

- At the same time, Jesus is changing us from within. He is purifying us by His blood through the mighty agency of the Third Person of the Godhead, the Holy Spirit (John 16:7–14; Ezek. 36:25–27; Heb. 8:10; Ps. 119:32; Rom. 8:1–4, 14; 1 John 1:7; Jude 24).

Soon He will come for us. Everyone will have made his or her own decision. They will have made their choice either to serve Him or not to serve Him (Rev. 22: 11, 12). Jesus will come without sin (Heb. 9:28), and take us home (1 Thess. 4:16, 17). He will give us new, incorruptible bodies, no longer subject to the cruel enemy of death (1 Cor. 15:51–55).

A PEN PICTURE OF THE JUDGMENT

Daniel 7:9,10,13, & 14.

- The Ancient of Days is the Father (Pss, 90:2, 103:19)

- The Holy Angels, thousands and thousands, ten thousand times ten thousand attend this great tribunal (Dan. 7:10; Ps.103:20, 21).

- Jesus comes to the Ancient of Days to engage in the last acts of His ministration on our behalf: to perform the work of the investigative judgment and to make an atonement for all who are found to be entitled to its benefits (Dan. 7: 13, 14) 9

- In the services of the earthly sanctuary, only those who came to God with confession and repentance, and those whose sins have been transferred to the Sanctuary through the blood of the sin offerings had a part in the Day- of Atonement. So in the great day of final atonement, *the only cases considered are of the professed people of God. (The judgment of the wicked is a distinct and separate work, and takes place at a later period).* 1 Peter 4:17 says, ". . . judgment must begin at the house of God: and if it first begin at us, what shall the end be of them that obey not the gospel of God?"

THE BOOKS WERE OPENED

- In Revelation 20:12, John, the Revelator mentions the Book of Life, where our works are recorded. Jesus told His disciples, "rejoice, because your names are written in heaven" (Luke 10:20). Since we, too, have accepted Jesus as our personal Savior, we should rejoice because our names are written in heaven, also. Paul mentions the Book of Life in Philippians 4:3. Daniel says that those with their names written in the book of life will be delivered from the "time of trouble, such as never was" (Dan. 12:1).

- In Revelation 20:15, we are told that only those whose names are not written in the Book of Life will be destroyed. The book of remembrance is where the goods deeds of those who feared the Lord are recorded (Mal. 3:16). Every righteous deed is immortalized. Every temptation resisted, every evil overcome, every tenderhearted word spoken, every tear of repentance shed, every tear shed for others is recorded there (Ps. 56:8).

Isn't God good? He sees the struggles we have, the

tears we shed, the end deeds we perform. He hears us when we pour out or hearts to him in love; he sees every deed of self-denial and he fulfills every longing after righteousness, which he imparts.

- There is a record of the sins of men: "Behold, it is written before me: . . . Your iniquities, and the iniquities of your fathers together, saith the Lord (Isa. 65:6, 7). "Every man's work passes in review before God, and is registered for faithfulness or unfaithfulness. Opposite each name in the books of heaven is entered with terrible exactness every wrong word, every selfish act, every unfulfilled duty, and every secret sin with every artful dissembling. Heaven-sent warnings or reproofs neglected, wasted moments, unimproved opportunities, the influence exerted for good or evil with its far-reaching results are chronicled by the recording angel" (*Great Controversy*, p. 482). The law of God is the standard by which the characters and lives of men will be tested in the Judgment (Eccles. 12:13,14; James 2:12).

IS THE STANDARD OF GOD TOO DIFFICULT FOR US TO REACH?

- It is impossible to reach without divine power, but we can do all things through Christ which strengths us (Phil. 4:13).

- Jesus is living within us (Gal. 2:20; Rev. 3:20).

- The righteousness of the law is being fulfilled in us who are led by the Holy Spirit (Rom. 8:1–4, 14).

- Jesus is our advocate (1John 2:1).

- He is able to present us faultless before His throne (Jude 24).

LESSONS FROM THE STUDY OF THE SANCTUARY

- Over the Law of God, which was contained in the Ark of the Testament, was the Mercy Seat where God's Presence was manifested as a glorious light. This light represented God's character (Exod. 34:4–7). Our Bible tells us that He is merciful, gracious, and long-suffering. He is love (1John 4:8, 16). He loved us enough to give Jesus to die a cruel death for us (John 3:16; Heb. 2:14). Jesus loved us enough to willingly pay the penalty of sin for us, since sin requires death (John 10:18). We repeat: God Himself paid the penalty of sin for us through the blood of Jesus! What amazing grace! (Rom. 6:23b, Eph. 2:8).

- Just as the blood of the Lord's goat cleansed all of the people and the Earthly Sanctuary on the Day –of Atonement, so Jesus' Blood will cleanse us, and even now is cleansing us from all of our unrighteousness (1 John 1:7).

- As we are accounted righteous by faith in Jesus so we will live a righteous life by faith in Jesus (Rom. 1:17).

THE FINAL DECISION

- The One who died in our place makes the final decision in each case. The Father has given all judgment into the wounded hands of the Son, who suffered a deep agony of soul for us, of which suffering we are but faintly aware (John 5:22, Isa. 53:3–6). It is amazing that the Source of all Life, the One Whose Life is original and un-borrowed (John 1:1–3), took a human body so that He could die for us, and thus destroy the works of the Devil (Heb. 2:14).

- He loves us, lives to make intercession for us, and is able to save us all to the uttermost (Heb. 7:25).

THE ADVERSARY

- The Devil is angry with us. The Bible describes him as a roaring lion who is seeking people to devour (1 Pet. 5:8), and he knows his time is short (Rev. 12:12).

- Revelation 12:17 mentions the wrath of Satan against God's remnant people, who are the last part of His true believers who are living just before Jesus comes.

- On the Day of Atonement in the earthly sanctuary, at the end of the purifying of the sanctuary, (Levi. 16:30, 33) the high priest confessed the sins of the people on the head of the Scapegoat, which represents Satan. Then he is taken out into the wilderness, where he eventually dies. In this picture we can see a mini-picture of the final destruction of the Devil.

THERE IS HOPE

- Our High Priest, Jesus, knows how to deliver us out of all of our troubles because He has gone through all that we must go through, but, even to a greater degree (Heb. 2:10, 4:14;). Because of His sinless nature from birth, sin must have totally disgusted Him in any form. He had no familiarity with it. He loved the sinner, but He hated sin because He knew the awful results of it, which results we, as fallen members of the family of Adam, are just beginning to see in its true light.

- He invites us to come boldly to the throne of grace to find grace to help in time of need (Heb. 2:16, Rev. 3:10, Dan. 12:1).

- The earthly high priest wore a breastplate set with twelve precious stones, each one representing one of the twelve tribes of Israel. Jesus carries our names on His heavenly breastplate right over His heart. It is comforting to know that every time His Divine/human heart beats, He is sending waves of grace and love to each of us. (The writings of the servant of the Lord tell us that there is an atmosphere of grace surrounding our earth as real as the atmosphere where the birds fly).

- Jesus looks upon the rainbow that encircles God's throne. ["The (rain) bow represents God's love, which encircles the earth and links earth with heaven.] As we gaze upon the beautiful sight, may we be joyful in God, assured that He Himself is looking upon this token of His covenant and that as He looks upon it He remembers the children of earth to whom it was given..." (Review and Herald, Feb. 26, 1880).

WE ARE HIS GEMSTONES

- Gemstones must be ground and polished to bring out their luster.

- We, as Jesus' rough stones, taken from the quarry of life, must also be ground and polished to get rid of the roughness and uneven edges in our lives and to make us into gemstones for His kingdom. Sometimes the polishing may cause pain, but the loving hand of Jesus is doing the polishing, and He will not allow us to go through anything we are unable to bear, because He loves us so much (1 Cor, 10:13). His job is to save us, not to destroy us (John 3:16, 17).

- One day, soon, it will be over and there will be a new heaven and a new earth, filled with righteousness. God will live with us, and there will be no more pain, death, sorrow or crying (Rev. 21:1–5).

ASK JESUS

- Ask Jesus to complete His High Priestly Ministry in your life (Heb. 7:25, 12:1, 2).

- Remember to pray and consecrate yourself to Him every day. (Lam. 3:22, 23).

- Remember that He loves you and will be by your side each step of the way. (Isa. 43:1–3, 63:9).

ABOUT THE AUTHOR

Norma Gully is the daughter of Pastor Norman S. McLeod, Ph.D., and Vivian Fortier-McLeod (both now deceased). She was born at Loma Linda Hospital, and was educated mainly in the Seventh-day Adventist School system. In 1955 she graduated from Greater New York Academy as class valedictorian and was given a scholarship to Atlantic Union College. Later she completed a nursing program at San Diego City College, and is licensed to practice nursing in the States of California and Hawaii.

She is the widow of Wilbur Gully, a strong church Elder. Together, they brought many precious souls to Jesus. To the Glory of God, between them they helped to start six churches in California.

She has been employed by church conferences to teach the Bible; and for over thirty years her specialty has been teaching Bible prophecies, which include Jesus' work for us in the heavenly sanctuary. She believes that the Holy Spirit has directed her mind to these studies, and has presented Sanctuary Seminars in Northern and Central California, New York, and Hawaii. Because of the strong interest of thinking people and, most of all, the direction of the Holy Spirit, she humbly presents these materials for your consideration.

We invite you to view the complete
selection of titles we publish at:
www.TEACHServices.com

scan with your mobile
device to go directly
to our website

Please write or email us your praises, reactions, or
thoughts about this or any other book we publish at:

TEACH Services, Inc.
P U B L I S H I N G

www.TEACHServices.com ● (800) 367-1844

P.O. Box 954
Ringgold, GA 30736

Info@TEACHServices.com

TEACH Services, Inc., titles may be purchased in bulk
for educational, business, fund-raising, or sales
promotional use. For information, please e-mail:

BulkSales@TEACHServices.com

Finally if you are interested in seeing
your own book in print, please contact us at

publishing@TEACHServices.com

We would be happy to review your manuscript for free.

www.ingramcontent.com/pod-product-compliance
Lightning Source LLC
Chambersburg PA
CBHW060808110426
42739CB00032BA/3147